HYDROPONICS FOR PREPPERS

The Complete Beginner-Friendly Guide to Creating Your Hydroponic Survival Garden | Live Off Grid with the Kratky Method and Become Self-Sufficient

Jacob A. Moore

© Copyright 2022 by Jacob A. Moore - All rights reserved

The content contained within this book may not be reproduced, duplicated, or transmitted without direct written permission from the author or the publisher. Under no circumstances will any blame or legal responsibility be held against the publisher or author for any damages, reparations, or monetary loss due to the information contained within this book. Either directly or indirectly.

Legal Notice: This book is copyright protected. This book is only for personal use. You cannot amend, distribute, sell, use, quote, or paraphrase any part or the content within this book without the consent of the author or publisher.

Disclaimer Notice Please note that the information contained within this document is for educational and entertainment purposes only. All efforts have been executed to present accurate, up-to-date, and reliable, complete information. No warranties of any kind are declared or implied. Readers acknowledge that the author is not engaging in the rendering of legal, financial, medical, or professional advice.

The content within this book has been derived from various sources. Please consult a licensed professional before attempting any techniques outlined in this book.

By reading this document, the reader agrees that under no circumstances is the author responsible for any losses, direct or indirect, which are incurred as a result of the use of the information contained within this document, including, but not limited to, errors, omissions, or inaccuracies.

Table of Content

INTRODUCTION 9

HYDROPONICS BASIC 11

    History 12

    What Is Hydroponic 15

    How Hydroponics Works 15

    Pros & Cons 17

TYPES OF HYDROPONICS 19

    1. The Wick System 20

    2. Deep Water Colture (Dwc) 24

    3. Ebb and Flow 27

    4. Drip System 30

    5. N.F.T. (Nutrient Film Technique) 33

    6. Aquaponic 36

WHAT WE NEED FOR HYDROPONICS 39

    Water 39

    Light 39

    Nutrients 40

    Reservoir 40

    Grow Trays and Net Pot 41

Tubes or PVC Pipe 42

Air Stone and Pump 42

Ph Meter 43

MONITORING AND MAINTENANCE 45

Monitoring 45

Maintenance 46

Why Ph Is So Important 48

MOST COMMON PROBLEMS 51

1. System Problem 51

2. Plant Problem 54

CREATE YOUR HYDROPONIC SURVIVAL GARDEN 61

Equipment Needed: 61

Step by Step Guide: 63

THE KRATKY METHOD (OFF-GRID SYSTEM) 65

Equipment Needed 66

Step by Step Guide 70

THE FASTEST GROWING PLANTS 75

CONCLUSION 81

INTRODUCTION

Day after day, preppers look for new ways to become self-sufficient. One of the things that will become essential after the world has collapsed around you is growing your food. You can't rely on the government to feed your family. Any major catastrophe will disrupt the food supply, leaving grocery store shelves bare and farmers' fields uncultivated. You have to cultivate your food all year long, and for some people, this will require growing food in areas without access to the fertile soil.

As the saying goes, man cannot live on bread alone or any particular type of food, for that matter. However, you may be able to survive for a while on stockpiled dry beans and rice, and soon you're going to start to have health problems due to vitamin deficiencies. Eating a tight diet is also just depressing.

Listen up, survivors! Up to ten times more can be produced using hydroponics than conventional soil farming. Greater Plant Size and a Greater Supply of Food. That means producing more food more quickly and not relying on traditional farming techniques for a family living in uncertain times. Additionally, you can do everything inside your house.

Hydroponic gardening is the practice of growing plants without the use of soil, and hydroponic systems are ideal for growing indoors. It's a practical method for growing a survival garden in the worst condition.

Most of the water that soil gardeners use on their plants is usually wasted. To ensure that the water reaches the roots, you must first pour more water onto the plants than they require.

Much of that water eventually evaporates after seeping deeper into the ground. This kind of water waste might not seem like a significant concern, but it will most definitely be when SHTF. This means you can grow food in a hydroponic garden without using up all your clean water.

HYDROPONICS BASIC

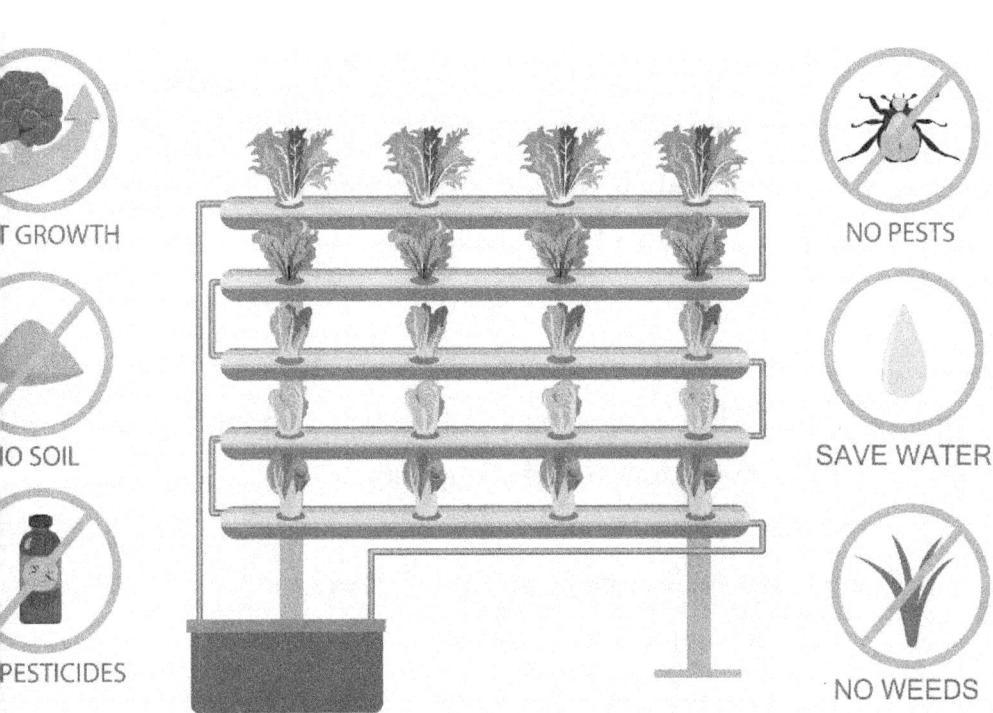

History

Hydroponics, or the cultivation of plants without soil, has a long history, dating back to very early civilizations and progressing to modern food production under challenging conditions or the cultivation of high-value items in regulated surroundings.

The earliest instances of hydroponics can be found in Babylon's Hanging Gardens and China's Floating Gardens. These strategies were utilized by humans thousands of years ago. Although the basic premise of hydroponics remains unchanged, new technology has enabled us to produce faster, stronger, and healthier plants.

Another example is the Aztecs' Central American floating gardens. They were a nomadic tribe who were forced onto the swampy shores of Lake Tenochtitlan, which is located in what is now Mexico's great central valley. Roughly treated by their more powerful neighbors and deprived of arable land, the Aztecs survived through extraordinary ingenuity. They decided to make it from the materials they had because they didn't have any land to cultivate crops.

The understanding that gave place to actual hydroponic technologies arrived much later. It wasn't until 1600 that chemist Jan van Helmont discovered that plants get their nutrients from water. Francis Bacon in 1627 and John Woodward in 1699 contributed to the invention of soil plant cultures in a liquid medium. This technology quickly gained popularity among academics. Sachs and Knop created the first nutrient solution in 1860 that allowed plants to be cultured, a method they dubbed "nutriculture." We can now properly speak of hydroponics, although the term was not coined until over 70 years later.

Professor Gericke coined the term hydroponics, which is derived from the Greek terms "hydro" (water) and "ponos" (labor). He was also responsible for popularizing and transferring the technology from the laboratory to a commercial setting. He made headlines by growing twenty-five-foot-tall tomato vines in mineral nutrient solutions rather than soil.

During World War II, American troops deployed overseas produced vegetables hydroponically to alleviate the difficulty of delivering perishable food to barren Pacific Theater islands and arid Middle Eastern regions. Iwo Jima and Okinawa, once blood-soaked battlegrounds, were transformed into nutritious gardens of life. Soldiers protecting crucial oil fields in the Arabian Peninsula ate vegetables produced locally in the harshest desert settings.

Evidence from early 1970s shows that Hawaiian pot producers were among the first to identify the benefits of soil-less gardening, possibly inspired by the island's porous lava rocks. Growers were so taken with the airy volcanic texture of these Hawaiian rocks that the heat-expanded clay pellets used in current hydroponics attempt to mimic lava rocks in terms of water retention and available oxygen for roots. Soon after, Californians became aware of these "herban legends," and hydroponic cannabis began to gain traction in the marijuana industry.

Hydro came of age in the 1990s, while those at the forefront continued to develop improvements in soil-free cultivation, such as aeroponics and aquaponics. A fine mist of fertilizer solution is constantly sprayed onto roots in aeroponics for highly robust growth. Aquaponics mixes fish farming (aquaculture) and hydroponics by rearing fish in a reservoir, where their excretions feed the plants. During the Clinton administration, advances in environmental control technology made it much easier to adjust indoor growth-room temperature, humidity, and carbon dioxide levels, bringing hydroponics to a whole new level of efficiency.

What Is Hydroponic

Through a process known as photosynthesis, plants transform water and carbon dioxide into glucose and oxygen to develop. This process is carried out by sunlight, and a substance called chlorophyll resides in their leaves.

There isn't a single mention of soil there, which is all the evidence you need that plants can thrive without it. They do require nutrients and water, which can both be found in soil. However, if they can obtain these items elsewhere, they should stand with their roots submerged in a nutrient-rich solution. That is the fundamental idea behind hydroponics. Although "hydroponics" refers to growing plants in water, most people define it as cultivating plants without placing them in soil.

Hydroponics might be your ticket to eating what you grow if you've always wanted to start sustainable gardening but haven't had the land, space, or weather conditions where you live

How Hydroponics Works

Hydroponics is a little more involved than merely cultivating in water pools because plants can't grow on water alone. Since plants require nutrients, hydroponic systems operate more effectively when supplemented with nutrient solutions and water with dissolved minerals.

The roots of the plants hang into this solution and consume the enriched liquid supported in pots or on small rocks.

Plants can grow more quickly than in soil when they directly access water and nutrients. Hydroponically grown crops can reach maturity in as little as 30 days, and occasionally even as little as 10 or 14 days, compared to conventionally produced crops that take 2 to 5 months or longer. Because of the significantly shortened growth period and the ability to grow crops in smaller locations and with fewer resources, hydroponics has been recognized as an effective technique for cultivating crops.

Anywhere in the world, regardless of the condition of the soil, hydroponics can be used. Since the single prerequisite is access to water, hydroponics is a flexible technique that can be used in rural and urban settings, making it an excellent option for individuals who live in deserts and those who reside in drought-prone areas locations.

Hydroponics can be used anywhere because there are no space or resource restrictions like traditional farming, hydroponics changes how we think about producing food.

Pros & Cons

Pros

- Water Efficiency

Growing plants can take a lot of water, and traditional agriculture historically wastes this resource. For instance, one apple uses approximately 14 gallons of water, but a single nut uses almost 5 gallons. Over 70% of freshwater worldwide is used for agriculture. Hydroponic systems use a lot less water than conventional growing techniques. Cultivators can only utilize the exact quantity of water necessary for healthy plants while growing in a climate-controlled environment. Overall, hydroponic farming uses ten times less water than traditional farming.

- Improved Growth Rates

There is a little misunderstanding when it comes to plant harvesting from hydroponic systems. People believe that hydroponics will result in plants that are larger than those that can be grown on soil. Hydroponics, however, does enable plants to realize their full genetic potential, thus, this isn't the case. Because fewer obstacles restrict a plant's growth, this results in more numerous and healthier crops.

- Pest Issues

Because hydroponic systems don't require soil, pests are less common and have limited entry points. It is more difficult for insects to enter the system and harm plants.

Additionally, lesser bug issues translate as little to no pesticide use.

Cons

- Water Diseases

While certain waterborne diseases are more common in vegetables grown hydroponically, these systems may lessen or even eliminate pest pressure. The most prevalent ones, including Pythium, which contains multiple water mold species, impact the plant's root system.

- Plant Deficiency

The soil protects against extreme temperature fluctuations and routinely releases and absorbs nutrients. Plants grown in hydroponic systems respond poorly to issues like nutrient deficits because no soil can serve as a buffer.

Hydroponics for Peppers

TYPES OF HYDROPONICS

1. The Wick System

The wick system is the most straightforward hydroponic plant-growing technology available, making it accessible to just about anyone. Because it doesn't use aerators, pumps, or electricity, the wick method is unique. Most wick systems embed the plants directly inside an absorbent material like perlite or vermiculite. Nylon wicks surround the plants before being submerged immediately in the nutritional solution.

For those enthusiasts of reuse and upcycling, you will find that these systems only require four components and that you can easily make a functioning system out of common household objects. The most challenging phase is probably deciding the material to use for your wicks, simply because there are many options.

The name alludes to the fact that these systems utilize wicking to provide a water-based nutrition solution to plant roots.

- **Reservoir:**

    To supply the solution to the growing media as effectively as possible, the reservoir should be placed as close to the growing container as is practical. It's preferable to position your reservoir so it's easy to access since you'll be topping off the solution frequently and cleaning it out occasionally.

    Your reservoir should be a container that blocks light to prevent algae and other bacteria.

- **Growing container:**

    A growing container might be a specially designed grow tray, a simple bucket, or a plastic container. This will include plants and the growing media, which may be placed in growing containers as a whole or separated into separate containers. To allow the wicks to travel through, you must cut tiny slits or holes in the bottom of the container.

- **Growing medium:**

    The growing medium for wick system hydroponics must be able to absorb and keep moisture well because this is where the plants receive all of their water and nutrients. The most common growing media for wick systems are coco coir chips, perlite, and vermiculite because of their low weight, good water absorption, ability to maintain the root zone's moisture, and ability to supply roots with an abundance of oxygen.

- **Wicks:**

Anything from cotton, wool, and felt to nylon, polyurethane, and other synthetic materials can be used as the material. Before use, thoroughly washing the material could increase its wicking capacity. While almost any absorbent material can be used to create wicks, if you intend to use your system for a long time, selecting something robust and rot-resistant is preferable. One of the greatest things you can use is fiberglass wicking, which is available in rolls or spools and is typically sold in gardening supply stores but can also be used to make candles and oil lamps.

Pros:

- Cheap
- No electricity needed
- Easy to build

Cons:

- Nutrient is not distributed well
- Only for small plants

2. Deep Water Colture (Dwc)

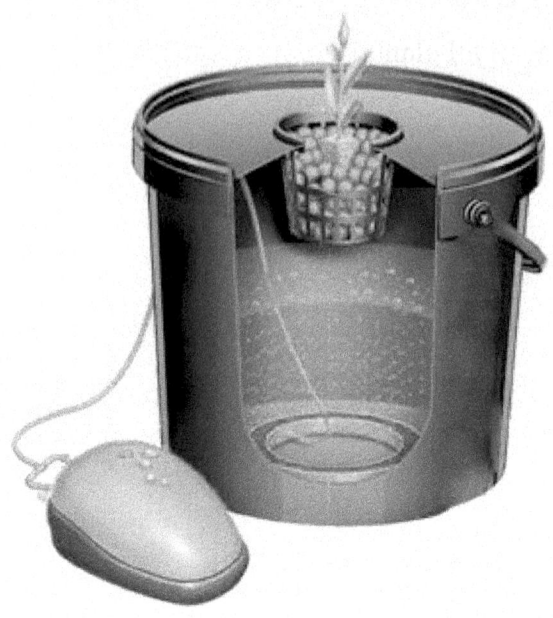

Plants receive everything they require from DWC's in a very straightforward method. The nutrition solution provides the plants with the water and nutrients they need. An air pump in the reservoir supplies all the oxygen your plants require. The last component is a light source that gives the plants the power they need for photosynthetic activity.

Only the above four components are required to build a hydroponic DWC system.

- **Pots:**

Net pots or plastic pots with mesh around the bottom and sides are typically used in DWC systems. Instead of being restricted to simply the bottom of the pot, this design enables the roots to emerge from any point in the pot. Additionally, the top of these pots will typically feature a lip, ensuring that they may rest on top of the reservoir lid and not fall into the system.

- **Reservoir:**

Your nutrient-rich water will be kept in this container. One plant can be grown in a modest setup with a five-gallon bucket purchased from a hardware store. You can utilize many other containers if you're developing a more extensive system with additional plants.

Choosing a dark-colored reservoir for your system is an excellent idea to prevent light from leaking in and warming the water. The lid should ideally be painted white or be of a light hue to avoid absorbing heat.

- **Air pump:**

This is essential in most DWC systems since it prevents your plants from suffocating. The air pump will give your plants extra support because there isn't enough oxygen in the water alone for them to live.

- **Air stones:**

The stone is connected to the air pump, which supplies it with oxygen. The hydroponic nutrient solution is subsequently oxygenated by the stone or diffuser's emission of microscopic air bubbles into the reservoir. The presence of dissolved oxygen in the nutrition solution is crucial because it prepares the nutrients for uptake by the roots

Pros:

- Roots are fully submerged
- Plants absorb nutrients quickly
- Suitable for all plants
- Plants grow faster

Cons:

- possibility of root disease
- daily maintenance

3. Ebb and Flow

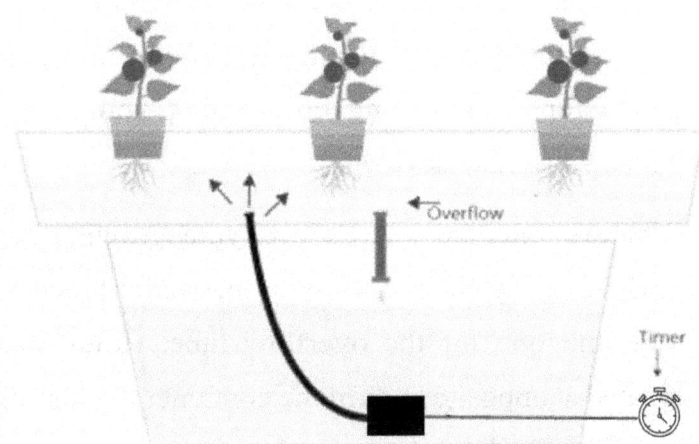

With this technique, you may quickly change your garden by adding or removing plants without impacting other crops. Like other techniques, the fundamental idea is relatively simple: Plants are placed in a tray, periodically supplied with water pumped out of a reservoir below, and are rich in nutrients. The water returns to the reservoir by using gravity so it can be utilized again.

The growing container, reservoir, submersible pump, and timer are the main components of the Ebb & Flow system.

- **Growing container:**

In a simple ebb and flow hydroponics system, you may either place your growing medium and plants directly into the holder or position your plants in separate gardening pots and let the growing media wick up the solution from the bottom of each pot. The disadvantage of growing all of your plants in the same container is that the roots might become intertwined, making it difficult to separate the plants for transplanting or cleaning your medium of diseases that may develop.

Whatever method you choose, your growing container must have two holes in the bottom: one for the inlet/outlet tube and one for the overflow tube. Holes should be located at opposite ends of the container to guarantee that the nutritional solution circulates throughout the period when the pump stays running after the system has been fully flooded. You should also guarantee that the inlet/outlet tube can operate correctly as a drain, which may necessitate tilting the growing container slightly to ensure this is in the lowest position.

- **Reservoir:**

To prevent algae and bacteria growth, your reservoir should be built of an opaque substance. Because the reservoir in an elemental ebb and flow system is directly below the growing container, a shallower container will work best. The reservoir size will be determined by the size of your growth operation and the sort of plants you intend to produce.

- **Pump and timer:**

A submersible pump is installed within the reservoir. Placing it right beneath the growing container reduces the vertical distance over which the nutritional solution must be pumped. You may use a simple pond or fountain pump if it has a high enough flow rate to fill the growth container quickly.

These hydroponics systems do not require a high-accuracy timer. Because the flood and drain cycles do not need to be timed to the second, a standard irrigation timer will suffice.

Pros:

- low maintenance
- Suitable for most plant types
- does not require expert knowledge

Cons:

- Not ideal for large plants
- Not the best for big plants

4. Drip System

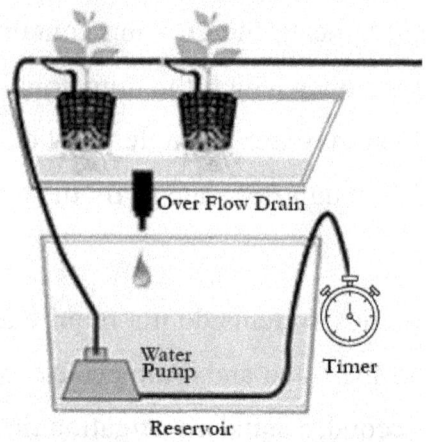

In drip system hydroponics, drip irrigation is used to supply the water-based nutrition solution to the roots of the plants. This low-flow irrigation slowly drips fluids at the base of the plants, preventing water loss due to evaporation.

Each plant receives a direct water supply and nutrients via the drip system. The solution is delivered to the plant directly through pipes and tubes from the water and nutrient reservoir. A submerged pump or gravity might be used to supply the water and nutrients.

Water flow can also be managed with the aid of a timer. So, by employing a pump and timer to transfer water from a reservoir to the plant, the system can be completely automated.

To set up a hydroponic system, you need a grow tray, a reservoir, a water pump, and drip emitters.

- **Tray:**
  In smaller recirculating setups, having all pots drain into a shared tray produces the most significant results. This is a more convenient solution than having separate run-off tubes from each pot to the reservoir.

- **Reservoir:**
  The reservoir will be a large bucket/bin. Depending on the size of your system, choose between 10 and 25-gallon volumes.

- **Water pump:**
  A standard submersible pump will be enough for the job. For modest setups, capacities ranging from 150 to 300 gallons per minute should suffice.

- **Drip emitters:**
  You will need to purchase an emitter for each plant, depending on the number of plants you intend to produce. They can be found at garden centers and hydroponic providers.

Pros:

- Simple to build
- very resource-efficient
- for any kind of plants

Cons:

- Dependence on electricity
- Drip systems are susceptible to tube clogging
- possibility of root diseases

5. N.F.T. (Nutrient Film Technique)

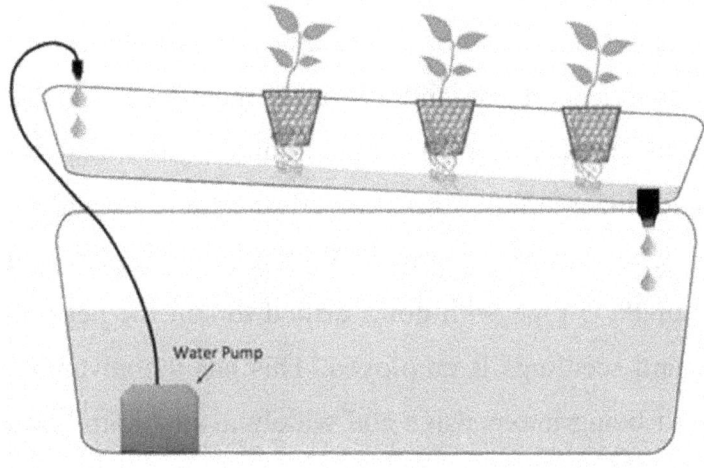

The hydroponics system known as the Nutrient Film Technique, or NFT, is well-liked and adaptable. The system uses a pump to feed fertilized water to the grow tray and a drain pipe to recycle the used nutrient solution, which is comparable to the Ebb and Flow method. The nutritional solution constantly flows over the roots of NFT, which is the difference. Gravity is employed to do this. A fresh solution is continuously pumped into the high end of the tube, and the grow tray is angled to let the water flow down towards the drainpipe.

You can create an excellent NFT system at home. The supplies are inexpensive, and the assembly is straightforward.

The components of an NFT system are:

- **Grow trays:**

  The Nutrient Film Technique employs tubes and channels for growth trays rather than flat trays. This makes it easier to angle it and ensure that the fertilizer solution runs directly to the roots without being wasted. In most DIY systems, a circular tube or PVC pipe with holes drilled to suit the net pots and seedlings is employed. This has the advantage of being inexpensive and widely available to home hobbyists.

- **Reservoir:**

  A pump on the high end and a drain tube on the low end links the reservoir to the channel in the grow tray. To oxygenate the water, you must additionally insert an air stone in the reservoir and connect it to an air pump outside. The NFT, unlike other systems, does not use an automatic timer linked to the water pump because the pump runs continuously. This can be a significant issue if there is a power outage, a blockage, or a system failure, so make sure to check the pump and fill the tube regularly and have a backup ready.

- **Water pump:**

    The nutrient solution is transported from the reservoir to the growing channels via a water pump and tubing in NFT hydroponic systems.

    Most growers like to keep their pumps running continually to provide a consistent flow of fertilizer solutions throughout their system. Others want to use a timer to assist them in setting up feeding schedules.

Pros:

- Mostly passive system
- Perfect for leafy vegetables

Cons:

- Mostly useful for plants with small roots
- Risk of spreading diseases from plant to plant

6. Aquaponic

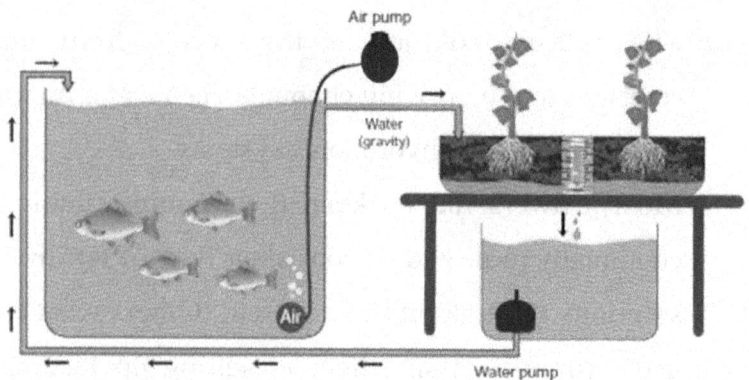

The cultivation of plants and fish in a recirculating environment is known as aquaponics.

Aquaponics is a plant-fish collaboration, and the phrase is derived from the words aquaculture (fish farming in a confined environment) and hydroponics (the growing of plants in a soil-less condition).

Aquaponic systems are available in various sizes, ranging from small interior units to massive commercial units. They might be freshwater systems or systems that contain salt or brackish water.

Fish consume food and excrete waste, which is transformed into nutrients by helpful microorganisms. Plants help to filter water by eating these nutrients.

Aquaponics is based on introducing food for fish, which serves as a start for the system. When fish eat and process this material, they produce urine and feces, which are high in ammonia and can be hazardous to plants and fish in large numbers.

After that, the water (now ammonia-rich) passes from the fish tank into a biofilter, along with un-eaten food and decomposing plant materials. Micro then breaks everything down inside the biofilter into organic nutrient solutions (nitrogen-rich) for growing veggies.

Pros:

- It has a high level of nutrient utilization
- Less water consumption

Cons:

- It needs electricity
- Complex system

WHAT WE NEED FOR HYDROPONICS

Water

Hydroponics is a Latin word meaning working water. Without soil, water works to sustain plant life by supplying it with nutrients, moisture, and oxygen. Due to its lack of dangerous contaminants, distilled water is the most recommended type for hydroponic systems. It works best when diluted with tap water. As an alternative, reverse osmosis-filtered tap water is another excellent option. If distilled water isn't available, we can use rainwater as well.

Light

Plants need light for photosynthesis, and sunlight is the best option.

If we were forced to stay indoors, we could still use artificial lights. The best choice for sure is LED lights; they have a low cost and long life, which means we can count on more harvests. LEDs have very low energy consumption and can provide the correct spectrum of light that our plants need.

If, on the other hand, we had a south-facing window, we could exploit the sunlight and still have good results.

Nutrients

To survive, all plants require nutrients. In conventional farming and gardening, the soil and other fertilizers like manure, compost, and chemical fertilizers provide the plants' nutrition. Since plants are not grown in soil in hydroponics, nutrients must be directly given through a watering solution.

Exists a standard recipe for these nutritional formulas? No, since every plant has varied nutrient needs. Additionally, various other variables, such as weather patterns and growth phases, have a role in this. Additionally, different hydroponic formulas have been produced. The primary nutrients that plants need are typically the same. Just the proportion of them varies.

One thing to bear in mind while selecting various options for your hydroponic garden is that you should only buy nutrients made exclusively for hydroponic systems. Forget about the multipurpose container that may be used in hydroponics and soil. Common soil fertilizers don't contain the essential micronutrients needed by hydroponic plants.

Reservoir

One essential part of hydroponic systems is the hydroponic reservoir. Water and fertilizer solution plants are needed for a healthy growth cycle to be kept in the reservoir. It enables the active or passive delivery of the nutrient solution to the developing plants.

Delivering the required nutrients and water to your developing plants while managing the nutrient solution's temperature, pH, concentration, and oxygenation is one of the critical challenges with hydroponics. When giving vital nutrients and water to your plants, a reservoir offers a significant volume of nutrient solution, which makes regulating these factors much more straightforward than any other choice.

Grow Trays and Net Pot

A grow tray is a container used in a hydroponic growing system to contain one or more plants. These trays may contain leach valves to allow water to drain out of the growing media when necessary, depending on the type of hydroponic system in use.

Some grow trays are intended to contain growing media (e.g., clay pebbles, coco coir, and others), while others are designed to hold pots with plants and medium.

A hydroponic tray is another name for a grow tray.

Net pots, also known as net cups or mesh pots, are basic webbed or slotted containers with holes of various sizes perforated along all sides. In hydroponic systems, net pots are frequently used because they provide optimal plant support and guarantee that nutrients and water reach the roots of the plants. They are a go-to item for fans of hydroponic farming since they are recyclable, sustainable, and environmentally friendly.

Tubes or PVC Pipe

One of the critical components of every hydroponic system is tubes. They deliver nutrients and water to your plants, allowing them to develop appropriately. No application will cause high-quality hydroponic tubing to leak or kink.

Tubes are essential in these techniques where it is necessary to have a pump to oxygenate or irrigate our plants.

Among the best materials that certainly stand out: PVC and plastic they have an almost unlimited lifespan and are easy to maintain and source.

Air Stone and Pump

Roots can suffocate without additional oxygen in systems like DWC, ebb and flow.

Hydroponic air stones and diffusers only really differ in terms of look and shape. They carry out the same actions.

As the name implies, air stones are a specific size and form of stone or cylinder. On the other hand, air diffusers can be shaped differently to perform more effectively and cover more ground.

The water pump powers your plants in active hydroponics. It's in charge of transferring the nutrient solution from the reservoir to the flood tray, which is home to your plants.

We need to cover the three main types of water pumps before we get into our list of the top hydroponic water pumps because doing so will make it easier for us to segment our list. The three distinct kinds of pumps are:

- **Sump pumps:** can be used whenever a bottom draw pump is required, however they are most frequently used in sump systems. They also aid in blending nutrients, which is beneficial!

- **Inline Pumps:** due to their strength and efficiency, inline pumps are frequently used, especially by growers with larger systems. They're seated by the reservoir.

- **Submersible pumps:** they are directly submerged in your reservoir and are ideal for hobbyists becausethey use less electricity.

Ph Meter

You may determine the pH of your nutrition solution using several different techniques. Some methods for calculating pH rely on color changes in particular organic pigments. These are visible techniques, like liquid test kits, pH test papers, and litmus tests.

By illuminating the sample and measuring the absorbance, photometric methods calculate pH.

Using the electrical potential of pH-sensitive electrodes as a measuring signal, potentiometric methods calculate pH. One of the most used types of pH sensors is the glass electrode. Starting with what a pH meter measures, we will then examine the mechanism pH meters employ.

MONITORING AND MAINTENANCE

Only a few steps are needed to grow hydroponic plants successfully once a growing system is operational. Keep in mind the 5 fundamental needs of plants while you perform the following checks on the system daily or every other day (light, water, nutrients, temperature, and oxygen).

Monitoring

- Make sure the system is functioning correctly by keeping an eye on it. Verify if it floods the plants and drains at a specific time. Small fragments of growing material can quickly clog the system's tubing, leaving your plants either "high and dry" or perpetually wet.

- Look at the plants. Is the growing media dehydrated, and are they wilting? Or is it wet? Adjust the nutrient solution's volume accordingly (this is for systems that periodically receive the nutrient solution, most likely through a timer).

- Keep an eye out for diseases, pests, and nutritional weaknesses. Treat any issues as soon as possible; else, they'll explode into far more significant issues than you might think.

- Learn to distinguish between good and bad bugs.

Encourage the presence of dragonflies, spiders, and ladybirds since they consume unwelcome insects. I adore ladybirds because I've seen them eat aphids.

Maintenance

- To begin, you should be aware that we will discuss two distinct sorts of water changes in hydroponics. The first category involves modest water changes, also known as 'topping off.' The next stage is bigger water changes, which occur considerably less frequently. Water changes are an essential aspect of hydroponic system maintenance. As your plants absorb fertilizer solution, the water level in your reservoir will decrease somewhat. Some water will evaporate from the fertilizer solution, lowering the water level. The water level will drop at varying rates based on the size of your system, the temperature and humidity in your grow room, and other factors. Whether or not you cover your reservoir (which I recommend if you don't have your grow tray immediately over your system) and even the growth cycle of your plants. That is why it is essential to inspect your reservoir daily. When you observe a drop in your reservoir's water level, it's time to add additional water and 'top up your reservoir.

- A clean system ensures healthier plants and less chance of obtaining sick plants. Of course, when your plants are actively developing, you'll clean your reservoir most of the time. This keeps the water pure and protects your plants from chemical harm and imbalance. You should clean your hydroponic reservoir every 2 to 6 weeks. This depends on how frequently you need to add and replace water and the size of your system. Sterilization is distinct in that it destroys all bacteria. You'll sanitize your system after each harvest or after significant insect and pathogen problems. You can clean your hydroponic reservoir using a solution of hydrogen peroxide and water or with a solution of vinegar and water. If you have plants growing in your system, try to avoid using chemicals. If you decide to use chemicals, ensure that they are thoroughly flushed and that no extra remains if you use hydrogen peroxide, dilute it in a 2:1 ratio with water. Use a lower concentration of peroxide. Just be sure to use food-grade hydrogen peroxide. If you're using vinegar, dilute it with water in a 1:1 ratio. Vinegar is an excellent organic cleaner, and the odor dissipates rapidly.
- Keep the dead matter trimmed because it depletes

a plant's energy and can be the start of a disease or pest problem.

- Add water to your nutrition solution as it starts to evaporate to bring it back to the proper level. Never add a little bit more nutrient powder to replace what you believe has been consumed. This is a really effective approach to destroying your plants.

Why Ph Is So Important

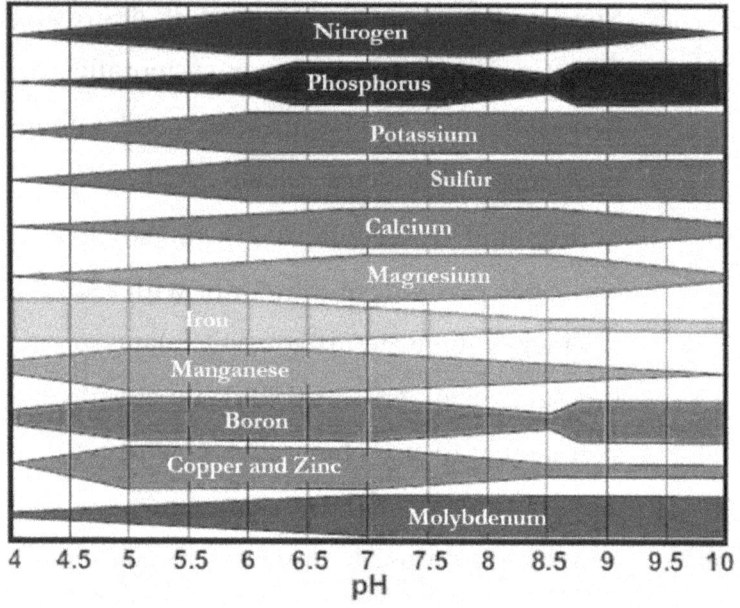

A scale known as pH is used to determine how acidic or alkaline a water-based solution is. Because it counts the number of hydrogen ions in a solution, it is often referred to as "power of hydrogen" or "potential hydrogen." A lower pH value denotes a more significant concentration of hydrogen ions because the pH scale is inversely proportional to the number of hydrogen ions.

Your hydroponic system's pH balance is crucial to the health and vitality of your crop. Essential minerals and micronutrients won't be available for uptake by your plant if the pH is out of range. Nutrient deficits and, finally, mortality may result from this.

The chemistry of pH and nutrition interaction is complicated, yet comprehending the fundamentals is easy.

The graph above offers a visual representation of how nutrients are absorbed in various pH levels. When combined with knowledge of a particular plant's nutritional needs throughout its life cycle, this enables you to start adjusting pH levels during certain growth phases to maximize the rate at which specific nutrients are absorbed.

This is crucial for leafy green plants in particular since healthy leaf development depends significantly on micronutrients. Plants with low micronutrient uptake frequently have leaves that are stunted and undeveloped.

Plants will have varying pH requirements, but generally, a pH range of 5 – 6.8 is considered optimal for hydroponics. The majority of plants grow best in slightly acidic conditions.

After combining the fertilizers with the water, the pH of the hydroponic nutrition solution needs to be adjusted. The pH of the final solution will change if nutrients are added to pH-balanced water; therefore, you will need to make another adjustment. Save yourself time and wait to alter the pH level until your nutrient solution is prepared.

Using commercial pH adjusting chemicals is the most efficient method for changing pH levels in a hydroponic reservoir, but any very acidic or basic substance will do. In most cases, you will need to lower the pH of the nutrient, and a few drops of vinegar or lemon juice can easily do the job.

MOST COMMON PROBLEMS

Many issues with hydroponics may be avoided or dealt with successfully. That's why it's crucial to learn how to do so. One of the greatest ways to do this is to learn from your mistakes. I've compiled the most frequent problems you might encounter. Hopefully, this knowledge will help you avoid some mistakes and arm you with the skills to handle others. These problems and their solutions can be divided into two groups:

1. System Problem

This group contains the most common system-related problems that you may experience.

System Clogging

Problem:

System clogging is the most frequent issue in hydroponic systems, particularly in a drip system. Growing medium fragments can clog the tubes. Clogging negatively impacts the system's circulation and seriously harms your crops.

Solution:

To avoid clog development, regularly rinse the tubes with warm water. You can also go from loose to heavy growing media, such as expanded clay.

System Leaks

Problem:

There are many different causes of system leakage. Any joints or valves in your system are susceptible to leaks. They can also happen if your system becomes obstructed, as occurs when a root mass clogs an NFT system and causes water to back up and overflow. If you design a system with a reservoir that can't hold all of the nutritional solutions in the system, leaks could also happen. In this situation, a power outage or pump failure could cause your reservoir to overflow and back up.

Solution:

Before you plant anything, test your system. Tighten any valves and ensure that all connections are secure. Check your system on a routine basis for issues such as root overgrowth, clogged drains, or outlets. Choose a reservoir that can comfortably hold all the nutrient solutions in the system, not just the amount in it when it is in use.

Algae Infestation

Problem:

Algae can clog the hydroponic system and obstruct the overall circulation of nutrient solutions. Simultaneously, algae can absorb nutrients and oxygen from the solution, affecting plant growth and development.

Solution:

Controlling algae growth in the solution can be attempted by limiting sunlight exposure to the nutrient solution and painting the reservoir black. Overwatering the seedlings promotes the growth of algae on their surface.

Root Rot

Problem:

When pathogen carriers infect the hydroponic system, root rot can appear. To avoid this, you must first determine what caused the infection in the first place. The following are common causes of root rot in hydroponic plants:

- Pests such as fungus gnats and other insects
- Spores

Solution:

Keep the nutrient solution temperature below 75 degrees f and aerate the area. Make sure the system is sterile and disinfects tools and transplants regularly. Check the plant roots regularly and use dark colors or thick materials to prevent light from reaching the root systems and causing root rot.

2. Plant Problem

This group contains the most common plant problems that you may experience.

Deficiencies

Low nutrient levels are caused by a lack of nutrients or excessive salt buildup in your hydroponic system, resulting in low yield and stunted plant growth. Growers should also understand that just because a plant exhibits signs of nutrient deficiency does not imply that its solution is deficient in this nutrient. Excessive phosphorus levels can prevent plants from absorbing other nutrients.

Here's how to fix it:

- Flushing the system is the best way to correct any nutrient deficiency. Taking all the nutrients away from the plants may appear counterproductive, but in almost every case, the solution does not lack nutrients. A secondary factor causes the deficiency.

- Remove any leaves that have significant discoloration or are severely damaged to accomplish this. In severe cases, you may need to go all the way back to the stem. Removing any dead leaf matter is critical because rot allows pathogens to enter the system.

- Rinse the pots and grow medium with pH-balanced water to remove any salt buildup; the system should only be topped up with fresh water. At this point, it should run for 24 hours before measuring the pH and EC levels again. Once both levels have returned to normal, you can prepare a new batch, but only using three-quarters of the master blend dosage. As a final supplement, some organic liquid tea can be added. This benefits your plants without increasing certain nutrients to the point where the lockout occurs.

Pest

Many people believe that hydroponic gardens are pest-free, but this is not the case. While they are free of some pests, it is nearly impossible to keep pests away from a warm environment like an indoor growing area.

Unfortunately, plant pests have evolved to travel between crops, even if grown indoors. Growers must be vigilant because a pest infestation can quickly ruin crops if they are unaware of the problem.

The most common are:

- **Aphids:**

    Aphids are a common pest in hydroponic systems and can breed other pests such as ants, flies, mealybugs, and scale insects, all of which feed on plant sap. Aphids are frequently responsible for virus transmission within plants. Insecticides such as pyrethrin and insecticidal soaps can be used to control them. Aphids can also be controlled by introducing biocontrols into the system, such as ladybugs.

- **Thrips:**

    In hydroponic systems, thrips are a common pest. Thrips are small, thin insects that feed on plant sap. They are difficult to see because they move quickly and frequently hide on the undersides of leaves or between bud clusters. The most efficient technique to control thrips is to use physical barriers such as screens. Insecticides like pyrethrin and spinosad can be used to manage thrips.

- **Spider Mites:**

   They feed by piercing the plant's leaves with their mouthparts, causing cell injury that can result in stunted growth or even crop death! Spider mites can be found on flowering plants such as tomatoes, eggplants, broccoli, and blueberry, having a dull speckled look on the leaf's upper surface; when bad infestations occur, it proceeds to leaf chlorosis, which causes leaf drop. Spider mite numbers will expand due to the heat, while heat stress will kill off insects like thrips. When using an insecticide on spider mites, always apply it twice, 5 to 7 days apart, to achieve complete eradication. Because eggs may not respond as effectively as in adult stages, spacing out treatments is critical for the most significant results.

Diseases

Powdery mildew and mold are two of the most common diseases in hydroponic gardens.

- **Powdery mildew:**

When it comes to diseases that might damage your plants, powdery mildew is one of the most common culprits. Powdery mildew is a fungal disease that seems to have white powder strewn all over your plant. Fortunately, it is not a particularly dangerous disease, although severe cases can cause plant drooping, leaf yellowing, and even death. It has an impact on all hydroponic applications, both indoors and outdoors. Fortunately, it does not always spread to the surrounding plants. Low lighting, insufficient air circulation, and high humidity all contribute to powdery mildew. Surprisingly, it is more likely to develop on dry plants than on wet plants. This is because water will wash the spores away. Baking soda is the most often used therapy; however, it works best when combined with liquid soap and dormant oil. Spray 1 gallon of water with 3 tsp baking soda, 2 tsp dormant oil, and 2 tsp liquid soap.

- **Gray Mold:**

It's a fungus that can harm any plant. It typically attacks injured or dying plants, feeding on the nutrients available within the plant to grow. The plant is distinguished by white or gray "mushy" or powdery patches. It is particularly common in cooler weather with heavy humidity. Gray mold spreads readily from plant to plant. When disposingof gray mold-infected plants, place them in a brownpaper bag to prevent them from spreading to other areas of your garden. You can try using an organic fungicide to help control and eliminate gray mold.

How to prevent disease:

Most diseases may be avoided by managing humidity, air circulation, sanitizing tools, and using correct lighting.

- **Humidity:**

    High humidity is another factor that promotes the growth of most plant diseases. Humidity can be easily managed in an indoor hydroponic system using a suitable ventilation system or a dehumidifier. Controlling humidity in outdoor settings is nearly impossible. Your best bet is to guarantee proper air circulation.

- **Air Circulation:**

    Mold, mildew, and fungus spores are less likely to settle on your hydroponic plants when there is adequate air circulation. Properly spacing your plants while designing your garden allows air to circulate freely between them. Pruning plants regularly allows air to travel freely, not only between plants but also within the plant's leaves and branches.

- **Tools:**

Disinfect tools and equipment after each usage, and sometimes even between plants. This is especially true with pruning shears. Cleaning your instruments after each use prevents bacteria and mold from forming on plant leftovers, which are then transferred to your healthy plants the next time you use them. Vinegar is a powerful disinfectant. Using vinegar to clean your instruments is a natural approach to destroying bacteria without using harsh chemicals. You can also make a bleach solution to use as a powerful disinfectant. This solution will be effective at killing everything when adequately diluted. For 1 gallon of water, I personally use 1/3 of a cup of bleach. Remember to rinse very well if you use bleach or other chemicals in your garden. We absolutely must prevent our crops from being contaminated.

CREATE YOUR HYDROPONIC SURVIVAL GARDEN

If you have electricity Deep Water Culture is one of the most user-friendly, low-maintenance, and cost-effective hydroponic growth systems available.

Equipment Needed:

Before we get started, here are the components needed for a simple DWC hydroponic setup:

Reservoir:

You can use a plastic container with a lid (opaque as much as possible to avoid algae). We can plant a big single plant like tomato or use it for multiple smaller plants like green leafy vegetables.

Air Pump and Tubing:

A good aquarium air pump is crucial for oxygenating plants and keeping them from drowning. This plastic tubing will transport oxygen from the air pump to the nutritional solution. We can also use an air stone, but it is not strictly necessary.

Gravel:

Any substrate will do the job, but if we have availability in the environment around us of gravel, we may well use that. Gravel should be washed well, especially if it is collected outside.

Pot:

The optimal choice is definitely to use a net pot, but if we don't have any, we can use an ordinary pot and drill 10 or 15 holes on the sides

Hydroponics for Peppers

Step by Step Guide:

1) If your container is not light-resistant, spray it black. This is significant because light promotes the formation of algae, which can damage your plant. Then you'll paint it white to reflect light and keep the water temperature low for the root zone.

2) Cut holes in the lid to accommodate your plant pot.

3) Assemble your air system. Cut a piece of the airline and fit it on the air pump. After that, make a hole in the lid or top of the container and stick the hose connected to the air pump. Run the hose until it touches the bottom of the container.

4) Insert the seedling or plant into a net container and cover with a growing medium. If you remove your plant from the soil, make sure to rinse it out first to avoid contaminating the water.

5) Add water and mix your nutrient solution according to the manufacturer's recommendations. The water level should be high enough, so the growing media is moist 2-3 inches below the surface and dry on top. After the roots start dangling down, you won't need to bother about the water level.

THE KRATKY METHOD (OFF-GRID SYSTEM)

When SHTF, you might be confined to your home in a survival situation with little access to outside resources, but that doesn't mean your nutrition has to be restricted or unhealthy. I am a strong supporter of indoor hydroponic farming as well as backyard growing at home. Water-based hydroponic agriculture doesn't need soil or direct sunshine. Therefore, setting up a fruitful garden inside a garage, basement, or shed with the correct tools is simple.

The easiest and most suitable method for us is definitely the Kratky Method. In contrast to other hydroponic techniques, the Kratky method doesn't need pumps or other electronic devices. This setup can be entirely passive in grid-down conditions if you grow indoors or in a greenhouse, where you won't even need grow lights. Although beans and tomatoes can be grown with minimal modifications, it is best for leafy greens like lettuce, spinach, and herbs.

Equipment Needed
Container

First, we need a container with a lid. The size depends on the size and type of plant we want to grow. Indeed, we have empty jars in the pantry. Great, we can grow lettuce or spinach in a simple jar with some rainwater; just add a little fertilizer and put the jar behind a sunlit window. In 30 days, we will have our first crop. For larger plants such as tomatoes or peppers, we will need a larger container and some extra attention. Fruit plants are more demanding in terms of fertilizer and sunlight.

Water

Water is a tricky topic with hydroponic systems. There is a possibility that you will have high levels of chlorine or chloramine if you reside in a region with treated water. Your hydroponic solution will be thrown off as a result, and your plants will die quite soon. Thankfully, there are a few fast ways to get rid of chlorine and chloramine. The container should be filled with water and left outside in the sun for 24/48 hours. Any trace amounts of chlorine will be eliminated as a result. It can be more challenging to get rid of chloramine: Cut a lemon in half and mix the juice with water, half lemon each gallon of water. Many of the effects will be mitigated by lemon juice. Water from a reverse osmosis system is the best as there are no substances or bacteria that could make the crop sick.

Nutrients

Any specific fertilizer for hydroponics is fine; personally, I use a master blend formula with Epsom salt and calcium nitrate; the dosage depends on the type of plant you are growing.

The most common Master Blend ratio suitable for all plants is:

- 1 Gallon of Water
- 1 tsp of Master Blend 4-18-38
- ½ tsp Epsom Salt
- 1 tsp Calcium Nitrate

Growing Medium

The purpose of the growth medium is to aid in giving plant roots the moisture and oxygen they require. It also holds the plant erect and supports the plant's weight.

The media's ability to maximize the amount of nutrient exposure to plant roots is another function. People will use nutrient solutions to moisten the growing medium. The fertilizer will be delivered to the root system through the wet media.

Gardeners who use products other than soil have less fear of pests and diseases carried by the soil. They can cultivate stronger, better plants as a result. There are many types of growing mediums; we will analyze the most widely used and the most widely available.

Clay Pebbles

Hydroton-expanded clay pellets were arguably one of the most widely used forms of media in the past. As their name suggests, these are manufactured by expanding clay to make spherical balls of porous substance. The best thing about them is that they are pH neutral and nearly never release nutrients into the water stream. Their spherical form and porosity also aid in maintaining a good oxygen/water balance to prevent unnecessarily drying out or drowning the roots.

Rockwool

Since it has been used for many years, Rockwool is well-known among those who grow plants hydroponically. Similar to fiberglass, it is produced by melting rock and spinning it into incredibly thin and long strands. These fibers are taken and compressed into a range of sized cubes.

Gravel

The same element is used in aquarium construction. Any gravel kind may be used, provided it has been thoroughly cleaned. Easy to clean and reasonably inexpensive. Personally, I think this is the material that we are most interested in.

In your hydroponic garden, gravel is a form of medium that is readily accessible and locally available. You might be interested to hear that they were among the earliest growing media utilized in hydroponic systems.

Gravel is ideal for your hydroponic garden since it has incredible qualities, including solid air circulation and water drainage. Gravel has excellent drainage qualities, making it almost impossible to overwater. However, they cannot trap water because of their high drainage property. You must continue to invest in a good irrigation system that will supply water to the roots of your plants.

You can use river rock as a substrate for your plants. They may not be the best option, but it's worth a try.

Be careful if you use gravel from a river; gravel could contain a lot of dirt or other debris. To stop these particles from blocking your system, they must be cleaned.

Another fantastic property of gravel is that it is infinitely reusable; just wash it thoroughly at the end of a harvest.

Step by Step Guide

To approach the Kratky method, the best way is to try growing a green leafy vegetable in a very ordinary mason jar.

Equipment

- Mason jar with lid
- 3-inch net cup
- 1 cube of rockwool or 1 jiffy
- Gravel or another growing medium
- Rainwater or reverse osmosis water or distilled water
- Nutrients
- Aluminum foil, paper or a piece of clothes

How To Proceed:

1) First, we need to take the metal circle off the Mason jar lid, leaving the metal sealing ring in place. Take one of your net cups, and you'll discover that it easily fits into the jar's top without falling in.

2) To ensure we correctly apply the Kratky approach, we will need to mark an appropriate fill line. This means that we must draw a point with a permanent marker at the height of 1/4 above the bottom of our Net cup.

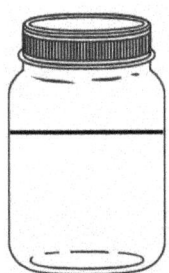

3) This step is unnecessary if you choose to use an amber Mason jar, but if you have a clear jar, we'll need to paint it or cover it in some other way (foil on the outside or even opaque tape will do the trick). This is due to the possibility of mildew or germs being produced by sunlight penetrating our nutrient solution from the inside, which we definitely do not want. If you prefer, you may just wrap the outside of the mason jar in foil. We only need to make sure that sunlight doesn't get inside.

4) Mix up your nutrient solution and pour it into your Kratky jar up to the fill line.

5) Soak your rockwool cube or jiffy with the nutrient solution and put into the net cup.

6) Fill the space between the rockwool cube and the net cup with washed gravel.

7) Add 2 – 3 seeds from the plant which you selected in the rockwool cube.

Useful Tips:

We can make a mini-greenhouse to promote germination by taking a transparent plastic bag. Simply put it over the top of our Kratky jar to cover it loosely. This will enable us to create enough humidity to promote healthy germination and allow the roots to seek water and nutrients independently.

To ensure that the nutrients are continually in contact with the roots and that your plant is receiving nutrients, you should keep an eye on the levels of your nutritional water. But it's only enough to keep a portion of your roots covered; don't fill it all the way.

If you plant spinach, lettuce or other green leaf plants, after about 30 days you can harvest your first crop.

THE FASTEST GROWING PLANTS

Growing plants that will mature and be ready for harvest in a short amount of time is crucial for a prepper. We've compiled a list of the top hydroponic plants that grow quickly and produce a speedy, high-quality harvest.

Kale

It is one of the foods with the highest nutritional density on the planet, and hydroponically growing it boosts its nutritious value even more.

Watercress

It makes sense that watercress, an aquatic plant, would work well in hydroponic systems. You might be shocked to learn that watercress is the oldest leafy vegetable that humans are known to have ingested. You can grow it from seeds or cuttings that form roots in nutrient-rich water in a few days. Once the watercress plant's roots have grown, move them into a hydroponic system.

Spinach

For a good reason, spinach has risen to the top of the list of superfoods. Spinach offers a wide range of health advantages due to its high iron, zinc, manganese, and magnesium content. Compared to spinach grown in the soil, spinach produced in a hydroponic system yields a greater quantity of high-quality leaves. In a hydroponic system, spinach, one of the vegetable crops with the best yields, can be harvested after 15 to 20 days.

Swiss Chard

Swiss chards can be harvested in about 35 days. Even after being harvested, it will keep growing, prospering, and producing a large crop. Although it can handle most temperatures and is exceedingly adaptable, the plant does best in cooler climates.

Lettuce

A great component of the salad sandwich in your home, lettuce is arguably the vegetable grown most frequently in hydroponic systems. They grow pretty quickly in a hydroponic setup and are relatively simple to care for. Any hydroponics system, such as the NFT, Aeroponics, Ebb & Flow, etc., can be used to grow lettuce. If you simply begin with hydroponics, this vegetable is, without a doubt, a great plant.

Tomatoes

Both commercial growers and hydroponic hobbyists have cultivated a variety of tomatoes. The tomato is a fruit according to botany, but most people—both buyers and sellers—consider it to be a vegetable. One thing to remember is that tomatoes need a lot of light. So, if you want to grow indoors, be prepared to buy some grow lights.

Cucumbers

Under ideal circumstances, they develop quickly and produce very high yields. Cucumbers come in all shapes and sizes. Everyone can thrive in hydroponics. As a warm-climate plant, the cucumber needs adequate light and temperature.

Blueberries

Hydroponics is an excellent way to cultivate blueberries, a delicious fruit full of vitamins for your meal. Often not until the second year, this plant takes longer than strawberries to produce fruit. Typically, they are raised in an NFT system. Blueberries are difficult to grow from seeds, thus, transplants are advised.

Strawberry

Hydroponic gardening is ideal for strawberries. These fruits are one of the most widely produced plants in industrial hydroponic production. Commercial farms have been growing in large-scale NFT systems for a long time. However, cultivating strawberries at home and picking the fruits all year long may still enjoy delectable fresh strawberries to feed your entire family.

Arugula

Another type of leafy green develops more quickly in a hydroponic system than in soil. For its sour/peppery flavor, arugula leaves are used in various culinary preparations. With hydroponic systems, this quickly growing plant can be harvested in as little as 30 days!

Beans

For your hydroponic garden, these are another fruitful and incredibly low-maintenance alternative. Since beans are a common ingredient in meals, growing them at home will guarantee that you have access to the vegetable whenever you need them. Trellis is required if you want to grow poles or string beans in your hydroponic garden. By doing this, the plants will be adequately supported when they need it most. Harvesting can begin somewhere between six- and eight weeks following germination, which can take anywhere between three and eight days. After harvesting is complete, you can let the crop grow for an additional three to four months. Keep in mind that beans do best in warm climates.

Radishes

When grown hydroponically, radishes provide the highest plant yield and are frequently chosen as a root crop. The only issue is that they could require some extra support from stakes and strings.

Watermelon

Watermelon is one of the fruit varieties that develops the fastest when planted hydroponically, despite not being the first fruit that comes to mind when considering plants grown in hydroponic systems. It takes about 10 to 12 weeks from seed to harvest.

Bok Choy

Bok Choy, sometimes called Chinese Cabbage, enjoys being in the water and can tolerate various temperatures. Because of this, it is an excellent complement to hydroponic systems that grow multiple crops. To keep it growing, you can only harvest a small number of leaves at once

Cabbage

This crop is easy to grow hydroponically and is a staple food around the world. The only issue you'll need to be on the lookout for is splitting, which happens when the head separates. Fortunately, it's simple to avoid; just maintain a steady intake of nutrients and water, and harvest as soon as the crop is ready.

CONCLUSION

According to the nonprofit organization Healthcare Ready, around 60% of Americans predict a big disaster affecting their families and households within the next five years.

More and more individuals understand that our exposure to everyday comforts has rendered us fairly vulnerable in the case of a catastrophe, particularly a long-term disaster that impedes our ability to just rush to the food store.

With all of the natural disasters and unanticipated calamities that have occurred in recent years, an increasing number of individuals are returning to the basics to ensure that they are entirely self-sufficient even in the most difficult circumstances.

This book covers the methods best suited to a survival condition.

In cases like this, we must be prepared to produce food with the resources at our disposal.

I focused on hydroponics because, in my opinion, it is the best way to succeed in meeting our family's nutritional needs while saving the most important resource we need: water.

The key to survival is to be prepared for anything. Now with the knowledge you have gained, you can begin to build your survival garden.

My advice is to start immediately, maybe with a jar and some lettuce seeds, and use the Kratky method. When you feel ready, get the materials and get into hydroponics. Even though we live in happy times and the supermarket shelves are full, you and your family will be glad to have fresh, organic vegetables available at no cost.

Thank you for purchasing my book. I hope it can help you to be more and more self-sufficient.

If you enjoyed and found what I wrote helpfully, I would be happy if you would leave a positive review. Thank you.

Always keep well in mind

THE KEY TO SURVIVAL IS PREPARATION

Jacob A. Moore

www.ingramcontent.com/pod-product-compliance
Lightning Source LLC
Chambersburg PA
CBHW071857160426
43209CB00005B/1088